FORGIVING THE UNREPENTANT

Ricardo "Ricky" Manuel

Pastor of Second Ebenezer Baptist Church Savannah, Georgia

Ricardo R. Manuel
800 Colbert Street Savannah, GA 31402
Phone: (912) 232-6810
Email: pastorrrmanuel@gmail.com

Ordering Information

Individual Sales: Ricardo R. Manuel's products are available through most bookstores. They can also be ordered directly from him at the address above.

Quantity Sales: Ricardo R. Manuel's products are available at special quantity discounts when purchased in bulk by corporations, churches, associations, nonprofits, libraries, and others, or for college textbook/course adoptions. Please write to the address above or call 912-232-7607.

ISBN-13: 9781722187828   **ISBN-10:** 1722187824

DEDICATION

I'm writing this book in dedication to my Beloved Daughter, the late Ms. Lorraine Marissa Manuel, Cuppie. Lorraine was born on Friday, November 20, 1987, in Savannah, Georgia. She was our second child and our only daughter.

To my wife, Angela: "You are more to me than mere words can describe, and I pause to honor you for being a great wife, friend, and more over the past 36 years. I could write a complete book just about our relationship, but I will save that for another time. We have been married now more years than we were single." I married her on my 21st birthday, December 4th, 1981. She was 19.

To my son, Ricardo E'ron: We call him Bubba. "You're a blessing, and without you, your mom and I would be a mess right now. You take a load off of our shoulders as we are growing older together, and I love you so much for the man you've become."

To my two grandchildren, Malorie Grace Manuel and Hraji Azaiah Franklin (Lorraine's Son) who call my wife G-Ma and me PaPa: "You are such a gift to me, and I'm so thankful that God allows me to have you in my life. You are Priceless."

To my late mother and father, Attie and Rudolpho: "I thank you both for bringing me into this world and for all that you did for me, my wife and children. You brought me to this party called life, taught me to dance, and insisted that it was up to me to continue dancing. I'm still doing 2nd Corinthians 5:7, walking by faith not by sight."

Trust

in the Lord 🖤

with all thine **heart**;

and *lean* <u>not</u>

unto thine own understanding.

in all thy ways

acknowledge Him,

and He shall **direct** thy paths.

Proverbs 3: 5-6

SCRIPTURES TO HELP

☐ *"Bear with each other and forgive one another if any of you has a grievance against someone. Forgive as the Lord forgave you."* **Colossians 3:13**

☐ *"And when you stand praying, if you hold anything against anyone, forgive them, so that your Father in heaven may forgive you your sins."* **Mark 11:25**

☐ *"If you forgive others the wrongs they have done to you, your Father in heaven will also forgive you. But if you do not forgive others, then your Father will not forgive the wrongs you have done."* **Matthew 6"14-15**

☐ *"You are the people of God; He loved you and chose you for His own. So then, you must clothe yourselves with compassion, kindness, humility, gentleness, and patience. Be tolerant with one another and forgive one another whenever any of you has a complaint against someone else. You must forgive one another just as the Lord has forgiven you."* **Colossians 3:12-13**

☐ *"Judge not, and you shall not be judged. Condemn not, and you shall not be condemned. Forgive, and you will be forgiven."* **Luke 6:37**

☐ *"Be kind to one another, tenderhearted, forgiving one another, as God in Christ forgave you."* **Ephesians 4:32**

☐ *"Then Peter came up and said to him, 'Lord, how often will my brother sin against me, and I forgive him? As many as seven times?' Jesus said to him, 'I do not say to you seven times, but seventy times seven."* **Matthew 18:21-22**

☐ *"So, if you are offering your gift at the altar and there remember that your brother has something against you, leave your gift there before the altar and go. First be reconciled to your brother, and then come and offer your gift."* **Matthew 5:23-24**

☐ *"Do not conform to the pattern of this world but be transformed by the renewing of your mind. Then you will be able to test and approve what God's will is—His good and perfect will."* **Romans 12:2**

☐ *"So, watch yourselves. 'If your brother or sister sins against you, rebuke them; and if they repent, forgive them. Even if they sin against you seven times in a day and seven times come back to you saying, 'I repent', you must forgive them."* **Luke 17:3-4**

☐ *"I, even I, am He who blots out your transgressions, for My own sake, and remembers your sins no more. Review the past for me; let us reason together; state the case for your innocence."* **Isaiah 43:25-26**

☐ *"If we confess our sins, He is faithful and just and will forgive us our sins and purify us from all unrighteousness."* **1 John 1:9**

☐ *"Repent, then, and turn to God, so that your sins may be wiped out, that times of refreshing may come from the Lord."* **Acts 3:19**

FOREWORD

While the death of our daughter has been the hardest thing we have had to go through, I would be remiss to let this time go by without sharing a few words of encouragement. I pray these words will minister to the hurt places in your hearts.

Words are Just Words Until...

People often say, "When life gives you lemons, make lemonade!" or, "When life throws a wrench in your plans, use the wrench to fix the problem." While these clichés are used frequently in life, they are just words. Life and it's many challenges are not quite that simple to handle. If we could just snap our fingers and fix our situations easily, we would never have let them get as bad in the first place.

Have you ever woken up one morning and said to yourself, "Today is the day I will no longer see my child? Today, I will no longer be able to hug her, kiss her, laugh with her, cry with her, or converse with her about anything." This happened to my husband and me; and I hope you never experience it.

Losing a daughter was not in my plans or in my husband's plans, but it happened. I've served the Lord for a long time and, I get that bad things sometimes happen to good people, but what do you do when the thing that happens is so senseless and unthinkable?

How do you reconcile Isaiah 55:8-9 that teaches, *"My thoughts are nothing like your thoughts," says the Lord? "And my ways are far beyond anything you could imagine. For just as the heavens are higher than the earth, so My ways are higher than your ways, and My thoughts higher than your thoughts..."*; and your experience? How do we prepare ourselves to be able to accept this tragedy? Is this His plan?

Many people try to comfort and to encourage when they are aware of tragic events. They say what they think they should say, but when you're living amid death and destruction, words are just words...

until you have to read your own child's obituary... until the Chaplin shows up to your address...

until you have to sleep in the room your child no longer sleeps in anymore...

until you have to explain to your grandchild that his mother can no longer take him to school or to the park again…

Again, words are just words… until…

Trust me, no one understands the deep anguish, frustration, hurt, and pain of losing a child unless they have gone through it—until they have walked a mile in your shoes. Don't let anyone fool you, or over-simplify this loss because it's different from losing any other family member. Why is it different? Because you had to nurture her, feed her, clothe her, bare pain for her, sacrifice for her, encourage her, defend her, and believe in her!

Even though God can prepare us **now** for something we normally would not be able to handle later without Him, you still must muster up the strength and the intestinal fortitude for the journey while going through.

Someone asked me, *"Please tell me how you really feel. I want to know the truth!" My response was, "You can't handle; and if I tell you, it might kill you!"*

There are only two choices in life after going through a traumatic or devastating experience: quit or go on with life! It can feel too hard to go on with life, but it's easy to quit.

Anybody can quit by simply stopping what they are doing. Anybody can throw in the towel, cave in, vacate the premises, depart from, resign, leave your position, walk out on, stand down, or shut down, withdraw from life, give up, cease all ties and communication with others, wind up, expire, or simply crawl under a rock and die.

All the above sound like good choices if you have ever gone through an emotionally disturbing event. And again, words are just words until you're facing the situations where you want to abandon this ship called life. Anyone can quit, but with God, everyone can keep on going.

We've all heard the adage, "Winners never quit; and quitters never win!" Again, they are just words when you're on the verge of facing nothingness (the absence or cessation of life or existence, or simply the state of being nothing).

Have you ever felt like your world was nothing and that all life had disappeared? Have you ever been so hurt that all you could see in your future was nothingness? When facing the death of a child, you can be one day away from a breakdown; one step away from losing it; one day from surrendering to the darkness and despair; but it doesn't have to end with you in despair. If you are in Christ, you may also be just one day away from a breakthrough; one day away from your deliverance. It's up to you to choose your outcome. My prayer for you, is like Joshua, you choose the Lord to serve during times of tragedy and loss.

Hall and Oates sang, "*She's gone... I better learn how to face it.*" Again, words are just words until you try to face death. No one warns you that you have to take your deceased child's toothbrush out the stand; no one warns you that you have to wash their dirty clothes, drive their car, check their bank account, or read their mail.

Don't let anyone tell you to get over it or that it's not that hard. It takes time to grieve and to mourn. The people who will say such things to you probably still have their children with them. Words are just words… until something happens; but I admonish you to be fully encouraged, if you're going through a similar situation. The only way out of a bad situation, is through. You must keep going, or you will just live in the horror of your loss forever.

We are not quitters, if we know Christ. We can use His grace and His strength to keep going. What if Jesus quit before Calvary?

What if your parents quit before you were conceived?

What if your spouse quit before proposing to you?

What if your child quit before commencement?

What if your pastor quit before he preached the sermon that God gave him for you?

Remember, stay strong—even in a quitting situation. Stay strong—even when the words become too hard to bear. God never quit on you. He gave you His word to sustain you through all the situations He allows you to go through. His words are the only ones that do matter. They are the ones that will strengthen you, because Jesus said in Luke 6:63, *"The Spirit gives life; the flesh counts for nothing. The words that I have spoken to you—they are full of the Spirit and life."*

The Lord also says in Isaiah 55:11, *"… so is my word that goes out of my mouth; It will not return to me empty but will accomplish what I desire and achieve the purpose for which I sent it."*

Read, listen to, watch on tv, share with someone the Word of God—even when it doesn't seem to make any difference in the pain you feel. It is working in you to affect change. You can make it. Don't give up, and don't give out.

There is no good reason for the death of a child. Satan wants you to become bitter and turn against God (Job 2:9). I am here to remind you that God loves you, and while He didn't cause the death, He can make something positive come from it. *"And we know that all things work together for good, for those who love God and are called according to His purpose"* (Romans 8:28).

Romans 5:3-5, declares, *"…We rejoice in our sufferings, knowing that suffering produces endurance, and endurance produces character, and character produces hope, and hope does not put us to shame, because God's love has been poured into our hearts through the Holy Ghost who has been given to us."*

"When the going gets tough, the tough get going". Well, the tough-in-Christ can keep going on—even when the words just don't make sense. Words are just words... until something happens.

~First Lady, Angela Manuel

ACKNOWLEDGMENTS

There have been many people who have helped me, and I would like to say a special thanks to the following people who have been there for me. If I forget anyone, please forgive me. All my fellow Clergy, I just couldn't list you all, but thank you for being my friends. The following people have been and are a great blessing to me:

- To all my Brothers and Sisters: the late William Manuel, Apostle Dennis Manuel, the late Annie V. Regustas, Ruby L. Bowden, the late Annie Florence and Leona Manuel, I love you all, and thank you all for being there for your baby brother.

- To all my Aunts, Uncles, Cousins, Brothers Christ, Sisters-in-Christ, and friends.

- To the late Bishop James & Mollie Hilton: I was nine years old when I received Christ under their leadership at The Fayetteville Deliverance and Evangelistic Center, Fayetteville, North Carolina. I truly thank God for The Hiltons.

- Pastor Thomas E. Williams, my Pastor here in Savannah Georgia. In 1992, I rededicated

  my life to Christ at First African Baptist Church of East Savannah. In 1996, I was ordained as a deacon. In 1998, I was licensed as a minister, and in 2000, I was ordained a minister under his leadership. I truly thank God for Pastor Williams. He sets an example that I admire; and I thank God for him daily. Love you Pastor.

- My deacon, Deacon John Roberson, I love you brother.

- Pastor Emeritus Harold Baker, Pastor Emeritus of The Second Ebenezer Missionary Baptist Church, Inc... Thank you, Pastor for many things, especially for bringing me to Second Ebenezer Missionary Baptist Church, Inc... I love you, Pastor.

- Pastor Larry E. Hilton, pastor of my home church, Fayetteville Deliverance and Evangelistic Center in Fayetteville, North Carolina. Larry was a childhood friend. I love you, Pastor.

- My Brother, Apostle Dennis H. Manuel, pastor of A Sound of Abundance Ministries and East Granville Street Church of God of Prophecy, both in Dunn, North Carolina.

  Love you brother, and thanks for all that you've done, are doing, and will do.

- My Brother-In-Law, Pastor Charles Roberson & The Kingdom Life family. I love you, Pastor. Special thanks to all the Sons and Daughters of Second Ebenezer: Evangelist Brenda Steadman, Minister Naomi Eason, Elder Cazzie Russell, Min. Samuel Treece, Min. Antonio Powell, Min. James Cooper, Pastor Alvin Petty, Pastor Artie Maxwell, and Pastor Earl Calloway, and Rev. Kinlaw.

- The late Deacon Willie Roberson, my Father-In-Law. Thanks to My Mother-In-Law, Mother Mary T. Roberson and All of my Brothers-in-Laws and Sisters In-Laws.

- Comforting Souls Ministry of First African Baptist Church of East Savannah, Georgia: Thanks for all that you've done, are doing, and will do.

- Last but certainly not least, all of the Officers and Members of Second Ebenezer Missionary Baptist Church, Inc. at 800 Colbert Street, Savannah, Georgia 31401. You have been and still are a great blessing to the Manuel family. May the Lord repay you all for what you have done, are doing and will do.

INTRODUCTION

Unrepentant means to me that a person doesn't care about what they have done, and they will not apologize-- knowing that they were wrong. Have you ever met anyone like that? If you have, my prayer is that I may help you deal with that person and not hold a grudge that can later become what the Bible refers to in Hebrews 12:15, as a "root of bitterness".

It is unfortunate that we must deal with unrepentant people in our lives, but hopefully my experience will give you the strength and the practical steps needed to forgive.

Trust me, dealing with an unrepentant person wasn't on my or my wife's bucket list of things to do in life. Who chooses that as something to experience? As a matter of fact, if I'm truly transparent, I thought I already knew how to forgive anyone. But God continues to enlarge my capacity to learn things at deeper levels. Forgiveness is one of those characteristics of Jesus that no one can tell you about; you must experience it through life's circumstances and choose to trust and obey God rather than your emotions and feelings.

An unrepentant person doesn't care about the damage they have caused, and they are naturally terrible people to deal with on our own; but with the help of God, we can forgive them.

We can't change what people do to us. In that sense, we are powerless. All we can do is handle our thoughts and actions about what has happened to us to make sure that they are Christlike.

The Apostle Paul reminds us in 2 Corinthians 10:3-7, *"…For though we live in the world, we do not wage war as the world does. The weapons we fight with are not the weapons of the world. On the contrary, they have divine power to demolish arguments and every pretension that sets itself up against the knowledge of God, and we take captive every thought to make it obedient to Christ."*

When you clearly understand this, you will be able to handle how you respond. You want a spiritual response and not a fleshy or carnal response. In fact, the Apostle Paul says that when we choose our thoughts, and make sure that they line up with God's thoughts as expressed in the Bible, it is then that we are using His divine power to change our feelings about the offense.

After the loss of my daughter Lorraine, the word unrepentant became more important than ever for me, because I realize that many people are unrepentant, and their behavior could entice Christians to sin, if we arc not following the Word of God.

It's tough watching someone walk around who has done something so wrong and so damaging to you and your family, knowing they will likely never apologize. It's the least they could do; but many will not.

I know forgiveness is tough, but you can do it. Don't let that dark place in your heart, keep you from living a life of joy. Yes, I have suffered other losses in my life: my mother, grandmother, grandfather, father, brother, two sisters, an uncle, friends and more have all died; but the loss of my beloved Cuppie was the

"Unrepentant means to me that a person doesn't care about what they have done, and they will not apologize, knowing that they were wrong."

toughest of them all for me to handle. Have you ever loss a child? It's extremely tough, but if you allow Him, God will help you through it. He loves you and wants to comfort you.

This book is to encourage those who have had positive words and prayers spoken to them after a loss, but who still can't seem to let go of the hurt and offense that seem to be so much worse when the offender is unrepentant.

This book will, prayerfully, help you learn how to forgive, especially if you're holding a grudge against someone. Am I telling you to get over it? No! It's totally out of line for someone to tell you that. Am I telling you that this will bring complete closure? No! What is closure? This is not television; it's real life, and forgiving is not for the weak or timid. It's for the person who wants to move forward in life whole and not bitter.

My goal is to share my experience in dealing with a tragedy that I never could have foreseen: the violent murder of my daughter and the unrepentant person who killed her. Hopefully you will find nuggets of truth in my story that will help you forgive someone who hasn't asked for forgiveness. Are you ready? Are you set? Well, let's go!

MY PRAYER FOR YOU, THE READER

Heavenly Father,

I come humbly before you to ask that the person reading this book will have a heart to receive this message of forgiveness. In the name of Jesus, I bind everything that would prevent them from receiving the healing that comes when we forgive those who have trespassed against us. Thank You for forgiving all our sins. I loose in them a receptive heart and ears to hear Your Holy Spirit as He minsters to them throughout this book. Help this book be a healing balm that ministers to every hurt, wounded, and broken part of their lives. Thank You for loving us and for forgiving us. Amen.

forgiveness is
not about
letting someone
off the hook
for their actions,
but *freeing*
ourselves of
negative energies
that bind us
to them.

TABLE OF CONTENTS

CHAPTER 1.

LORRAINE MARISSA MANUEL

L orraine was born November 20, 1987. Her first name "Lorraine" is her mother's middle name. Marissa is from her grandmother, Mary Roberson. I remember the day that Lorraine was born. We were so happy to have a little girl. I nicknamed her Cuppie. I have no idea what Cuppie stands for; all I know is that I held her in my hands like you would hold a little cup, and the name Cuppie came to my mind. I called her that from that day forward.

She was so sweet. Shortly after her birth, I had to report to Ft. Lee, Virginia for Basic NonCommissioned Officers Training Course. I tried to get out of going so I could spend more time with my family. I tried to get rescheduled, but the Command Sergeant Major informed me that I must report on the 22nd; and I did. The military was tough, and I really didn't want to leave my Cuppie; but I made it through.

She was an awesome daughter, and we had very little, to no problems with Lorraine. She was such a wonderful student who excelled in school. When she was in the third grade at Isle of Hope Elementary School, she wrote a book titled, *Alicia and Froggie*. Her mother and I were so proud of her. How many eight or nine-year-old children do you know who write books? That book is registered in the Library of Congress.

She graduated in 2006 from Savannah Arts Academy, a prestigious school where she majored in music. This was huge because it is the first dedicated Performing and Visual Arts charter school in Savannah, Georgia. Lorraine received the Hope Scholarship and later completed three years at Savannah State University.

On July 12, 2011, Lorraine had a son, Hraji. She was an outstanding mother, and she loved Hraji more than anyone else on earth. It was a joy seeing them interact. There are no words to express the love and joy parents feel at seeing the child they raised become a parent and patiently raise their grandchild.

She made her mother and me very proud.

As I think about both children, Cuppie and Bubba, I'm reminded of Psalm 127:3-4, *"Children are a heritage from the LORD, offspring a reward from Him. Like arrows in the hands of a warrior are children born in one's youth. Blessed is the man whose quiver is full of them"* (NLT).

At the end of 2014, Lorraine moved back in with me and her mother, and we were so happy. Happy because not only did we have her home again, but we had Hraji too. If I had it my way, everyone would live with us: my son, daughter, grands, and their spouses because I love my family, and I want to see them all every day.

CHAPTER 2.
THE DAY THAT WE WON'T FORGET

For many people out there who will read this book, you have unfortunately had a day that you won't forget. You suffered a loss; you have been hurt; you have been victimized; or some other tragedy has happened in your life.

Deep down inside the human heart there is a dark place, a place that nobody understands. Jeremiah 17:9 in the Message Bible puts it this way, *"The heart is hopelessly dark and deceitful; a puzzle that no one can figure out."* That word "heart' in the text does not mean your physical heart that pumps blood in your body. It refers to *the inner man, feelings, the intellect, the mind, or the will.* It's a place where the offended person goes in their mind that you must come out of because it's dark and will trick you.

The walls of that place are lined with bad memories and terrible thoughts of vengeance that the enemy of your soul, Satan, will use to torment you. He is a thief who comes only to steal and to kill, and to destroy you (John 10:10); but Jesus came to give you life, and life abundantly. You can come out of that dark place and live the abundant life!

Ecclesiastes 3:1-2 states, *"To everything there is a season, and a time to every purpose under the heaven: A time to be born, and a time to die."* These words we know to be true, and we all know that we are going to die one day; but when something unexpected happens and your child is killed prematurely, it really hurts and is so much harder to accept.

I've read Ecclesiastes 3:1-2 over and over; and I've heard Ecclesiastes 3:1-2 read over and over at funerals. My position as a pastor has had me to share this portion of scripture a lot. The challenge most face is, it doesn't matter who you are or what job you have, when something senseless happens, and a young person is killed, we all struggle accepting it, and it is especially hard because there is nothing that we can do about it. We can't go back and change what has happened. I know that we wish that we could, but we can't.

We live on an earth where people suffer from acts of violence daily; but if you're like me, you never think about it happening to you or to your family. I pray that you never have anything as senseless as an act of violence happen to you or to those you love. I also pray that if you have, you would read this book and find help to keep going.

I'm aware that we all deal with things differently, but walking around with bitterness in your heart and an unwillingness to forgive will create terrible consequences for you. *Bitterness is* defined *as resentful cynicism that results in an intense antagonism or hostility toward others caused by unfair treatment; or anger and disappointment at being treated unfairly; resentment; disagreeable; venomous.*

Bitterness can affect someone who experiences significant grief due to a loss. The negative thoughts that attack the mind after the senseless murder of a child can act on the mind and soul just like a poison acts on the body. Some poisons kill you instantly when you ingest them, but many of them work slower and over time—dragging out the suffering of its victim over a longer period.

Bitterness is a condition of the heart that is characterized by a person willfully choosing to hold on to angry feelings. It is these angry feelings that come from our angry thoughts. As we continuously think about the senseless thing that happened to us, we are taking the poison. The feelings that come after we meditate on the offense we've suffered long enough act as the poison that cripples us emotionally, spiritually, and physically. I know an older person who was hurt years ago, and the person who did the hurting apparently never apologized. This caused the person to be very bitter and angry. Being around this person with all the bitterness that has built up in their heart over the years is very taxing. It weighs down the people around you who want to interact with you. The longer you let the fruit of unforgiveness hang around, the worse things will be for you and for those who love you.

The consequences of constant bitterness will hurt those who are unwilling to forgive. I know you may be thinking, *"What about the person who did me wrong? They should be made to suffer because they made me suffer."* This is not about them, it's about you. God will deal with them, and you can trust Him. He won't fail you.

When someone takes the life of a loved one it hurts. The hurt is deep and manifests in ways that cannot be described. No one knows how they or any of their loved ones are going to die; and no one remembers being born. It just doesn't seem natural for a parent to bury their child, but it happens daily in the world that we live in.

I know that we never invite death, but we accept death easier when it's natural. We can accept it easier when a person has been sick or is old or has been involved in an accident, etc.; but when it's something like a homicide, we struggle accepting death. When someone takes the life of your loved one, it causes you to have so many questions. You wonder about the kind of life they would have had if they lived. Yes, we have struggles in life, and we must learn how to walk through the lows of life and still reflect Jesus Christ. This is one of the defining characteristics of a mature Christian.

Most people have no idea what has happened to you or how you deal with your struggles, but you can be a blessing to others if you share your story.

Your story may not be about the sudden death of a child. It may be about another tragedy, pain, abuse or other things you've suffered; but if you share it, others will be blessed. You might think I'm just saying this, but I promise you that I'm not.

Revelations 12:10-11 reminds us of some powerful truths, *"Then I heard a loud voice shouting across the heavens, 'It has come at last—salvation and power and the Kingdom of our God, and the authority of His Christ. For the accuser of our brothers and sisters has been thrown down to earth- the one who accuses them before our God day and night.* **And they have defeated him by the blood of the Lamb and by their testimony.** *And they did not love their lives so much that they were afraid to die. (NIV)".* When we share our story, we are sharing our testimony; and it has the power to defeat Satan! That's powerful.

June 4, 2015 started out like any other day. I was home in bed; my wife had already gone to work; and Lorraine needed me to watch Hraji for the day. No problem. It was right up my alley. Little PaPa and me together all day. I hugged and kissed Lorraine as I usually do before she leaves the house. She always said, "Daddy I'm not a baby"; but she will always be my baby girl. Yes, she grew up; but she never gained ground because as she got older, I got older and she was still my baby. She told me that she would get off around 3pm, and I said ok.

I didn't know that those would be the last words that we spoke to each other. They will always be special in my heart. Remember to always kiss your loved ones every day and tell them that you love them.

I didn't know if I would be home when Lorraine got off because I had little PaPa. Oh yeah, I'm PaPa, but I call Haji, PaPa. Please don't try to figure it out; (smile) it's a PaPa thing.

Lorraine called to check on Hraji two or three times that day, wanting to know what he was doing. The last time that I spoke with her, she said that she would be home soon, but she never made it home. Every day on earth, there are people who don't make it home.

I believe it was sometime after 3pm when I received a phone call from her fiancé, Marshall Franklin, that he believed, Lorraine had been shot. I panicked, and I argued with him because I didn't understand what was going on. Shot?!? There is no way to prepare for something like that! Why wasn't he with her? I was totally upset! I didn't know where she was. He explained to me that she was in a neighborhood in Savannah called Nottingham, at the place they were trying to rent. I grabbed Hraji, jumped in the car, went to Nottingham. Hraji showed me where to go-- he knew.

I never saw the place, and I haven't been there to this day. The shock of my daughter being shot was made worse because I wasn't even aware of her paying money to someone to rent a house-- she could have lived with us forever. I guess she was going to surprise me.

I left home so fast that I didn't even remember if I locked the house; I was in another zone. Yes, a three-year-old knew where to go, but I didn't. When I arrived, I couldn't get down the street because the police had it blocked off.

I saw the Public Affairs Officer from the police department who's always on the news. At that moment, I knew it was serious. Seeing the Public Affairs Officer is like seeing the Weather Channel people in your town-- usually that means that something bad is going to happen or has happened.

Yellow tape is also another bad sign and something that you never want to see. All that I could do at that time was pray and try to breathe!

I was hyperventilating but trying to stay cool in front of my grandson. I was told that Lorraine was in the ambulance, so I followed it to the hospital.

I called her mother on the way to the hospital; and we met there. My Cuppie; our beloved daughter, my son's Sister, Hraji's mother, and Malary Grace's aunt was shot in the head! We were devastated.

Although I argued with her fiancé, Marshall, the same night in the hospital, I love him. I hugged him and told him that this was NOT his fault. Ephesians 6:12 explains who is really responsible for this tragedy when it says, *"For we wrestle not against flesh and blood, but against principalities, against powers, against the rulers of the darkness of this world, against spiritual wickedness in high places."* Satan or his demons caused a lady to shoot Cuppie. Marshall loved Cuppie so much, and she loved him. He is very important to our family because he's Hraji's father, and he's doing an excellent job with him.

This was unbelievable!!! The five o'clock evening news had a story about our beloved daughter being shot, and the reporter said the shooter was in custody. I watch the news every day and never thought that one day my family would be the main story for something like this. I will never forget June 4th, 2015!!!

You may have a day that you will never forget, and I'm not asking you to forget it. I just want to remind you that as hard as the day was, God still loves you. He is with you—even if it doesn't feel like it. I am

13

only trying to help you keep on living by reminding you that you have a purpose, and the pain and anguish you feel will eventually subside. Keep going. You can make it!

Pray for those who insist that you "get over it". Why would anyone tell you to just forget it? Some people are cruel, and many are unthinking. Don't forget it; just refuse to let it make you bitter. Draw closer to God. Call on Him and ask Him to help you. He will!

King David understood how we feel when enemies are chasing us. He had a physical enemy, King Saul; but there are other enemies that come after us: works of the flesh like wrath, vengeance, bitterness, hatred, strife, and so many other spirits to attack us in our emotions. King David teaches us what to do when we are attacked by an enemy.

In Psalm 18, David cried out to God for help. Verse 3 says, "**I called** *on the LORD, who is worthy of praise,* *and* **He saved me** *from my enemies. The ropes of death* *entangled me; floods of destruction swept over me… death laid* *a trap in my path.* **But in my distress, I cried out to** **the LORD… He heard me from His** **sanctuary; my cry reached His ears**…*Then the* *earth quaked and trembled. The foundations of the mountains* *shook;* **they** quaked because of His anger. *Smoke poured from His nostrils; fierce flames leaped from His mouth. Glowing coals blazed from Him.* **HE OPENED THE HEAVENS AND CAME DOWN**...*Mounted on a mighty angelic being; He flew; soaring on the wings of the wind.* **He shrouded Himself in darkness, veiling His approach with dark rain clouds**... *He shot His arrows and scattered His enemies*... **He reached down from heaven and rescued me; He drew me out of deep waters. HE RESCUED ME FROM MY POWERFUL ENEMIES, FROM THOSE WHO HATED ME AND WERE TOO STRONG FOR ME... They attacked me at a moment when I was in distress, but the LORD supported me.** *He led me to a place of safety; He rescued me because He delights in me*... **The LORD rewarded me for doing right**; *He restored me because of my innocence*... **For I have kept the ways of the LORD; I have not turned from my God to follow evil... I have kept myself from sin (NLT)**"

There is so much in this Psalm that will minister to you. David had been anointed by God to be King, and the then current king, Saul, was jealous and fearful of being replaced, so he hunted David relentlessly trying to kill him. David refused to harm

King Saul because he was God's anointed king; instead, he ran for his life.

He wrote Psalms 18 at a time when he was on the run from that king of Israel. He didn't do anything wrong. Really, he was the victim, and yet he had to flee his home. Has anything bad ever happened to you, and you didn't do anything to cause it? If it has, I hope you will read Psalms 18 slowly, and ask God to help you.

When you've been hurt badly and the offender refuses to repent, it can feel as if the very Fruit of God's Spirit (love, joy, peace, patience, kindness, goodness, faithfulness, gentleness, and self-control) living in your born-again spirit are being hunted down by the works of the flesh (adultery, fornication, uncleanness, lewdness, idolatry, sorcery, hatred, contentions, jealousies, outburst of wrath, selfish ambitions, disagreements that lead to discord, heresies, envy, murders, drunkenness, revelries, and the like) . It can seem as if the only emotions that exist are the enemies of your faith; yet what can you do?

I'll tell you what you should do. Cry out to the LORD just like David did. He will hear you and come to your rescue. He doesn't want the enemies of your spirit, soul, and body to have control over you. David knew that some enemies were too powerful for him to handle alone, so he sought God. You must choose to be like David, and first recognize that you need help.

When you have experienced tragedies with unrepentant people, your emotions can be all over the place. This is true whether you are a pastor, a president, a mechanic, or a stay-at-home mom. We are humans with feelings. Without God, our natural responses are usually to get even for the offenses we suffered. That's why it is important to stay close to God in prayer and to stay close to other Christians who will help keep you lifted in prayer.

If you do what David did and keep yourself from sin by keeping your eyes fixed on God's word and His ways, He will vindicate you even if the criminal justice system does not. God loves you, and He cares about you! Cry out to Him and let Him rescue you.

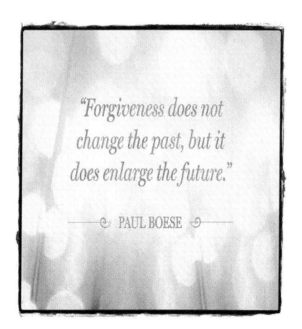

"Forgiveness does not change the past, but it does enlarge the future."

— PAUL BOESE —

CHAPTER 3.

PEOPLE

When things happen in your life, people will talk, speculate, spread rumors, and more. They can't resist trying to figure out, why it happened to you. Many are like Job's friends who came to him and accused him of doing something wrong to bring about the bad things that happened to him. *"You must have done something Job!"*

I'm writing to you out there to let you know that they are just being people. Bad things happen to people every day, and it has nothing to do with doing wrong. There is a devil in the world who loves to steal, to kill, and to destroy humans because as Revelations 12 states, *"...woe to the earth and the sea, because the devil has gone down to you! He is filled with fury, because he knows that his time is short."*

People who know little and talk much have spread many rumors, and it's a shame. You really don't have to worry about them because they will never say anything in your face.

You went through pain, suffering, hurt, and

"You are blessed, and it wasn't your fault!"

devastation; and all they can do is say that you must have done wrong? Let me comfort you on today. **You don't have to do anything wrong for something bad to happen to you.** Please know that. I want to encourage you to ignore what they say. Focus on what God says.

People die every day because of senseless acts done by people under the influence of Satan. Again, let me remind you of what Ephesians 6:12 says, *"For we are not fighting against flesh and blood enemies, but against evil rulers and authorities of the unseen world, against mighty powers in this dark world, and against evil spirits in the heavenly places* (NLT)." Don't let them make you feel guilty about what has happened to you or your family. There are spiritual forces that influence and harass people to do terrible things. The sad truth is that most people are not even aware that demonic forces are working against them through people. You don't have to be ignorant of how the devil works.

Bless those who curse you; pray for those who mistreat you and who insult you (Luke 6:28). It really works to change how you feel.

Please forgive them too, and continue to walk by faith and not by sight. You're blessed, and it wasn't your fault! You are blessed, and you are not cursed! You are blessed, and God loves you! You are blessed because you are the head and not the tail. You are blessed, and better days are on the way. Don't give up! You can make it. Keep going!

The devil wants you to stay in a dark place in your mind and emotions, but I am telling you to come out and live! You may feel like you're dead on the inside because you have been in that dark place for so long, but I'm here to tell you today like Jesus said to Lazarus after he had been dead for four days, "You, Come Forth!" You shall live and not die; and declare the works of the Lord (Psalms 118:17)!!!

> "When you hold resentment toward another, you are bound to that person or condition by an emotional link that is stronger than steel. Forgiveness is the only way to dissolve that link and get free."
>
> — ❧ CATHERINE PONDER ❧ —

CHAPTER 4.
LIFE AT THE HOSPITAL

We spent six days and nights at Memorial Hospital's Trauma Center. I have prayed with family members and for others in trauma, but now others were praying for me. The staff and employees were extremely nice to us and those who had loved ones in trauma.

I found out during this time, just how well our family was connected to people all over the world and how much we are loved. It humbled me then and now; and I can take no credit for it. God gets all the glory!

There were so many family members and friends visiting at the hospital that we were asked to move to another waiting area in the hospital that could accommodate all the people. One nurse asked if all the people were there for just one person.

We didn't have to worry about a thing at the hospital. Food was brought on a continuous basis-- so much that we had to share with others because often we didn't feel like eating. It was overwhelmingly beautiful how much love was poured out on our family.

The deacons, deaconesses, ministers, the entire family, and friends of Second Ebenezer, circled the wagons around us, and made sure that someone was at the hospital 24-hours a day. We had an aroundthe-clock guard. This must have been how Nehemiah felt as he was re-building the walls that surrounded Jerusalem in Nehemiah 1:1 – 7:73. God is faithful to provide us what we need. He is good and cares for us!

You need a good support group around you when you're going through traumatic times. Do you know who you can count on? Do you have a support team? Jesus came, according to Matthew 20:28, to serve and not to be served. That is the principle upon which my wife and I have built our ministry. We wanted to serve others and not to be served. In the 3rd chapter of John, Jesus washed His disciples' feet. We were used to serving/washing the feet of others, but now they were serving and doing for us. Luke 6:31 states, *"Do unto others as you would have them do to you."* If either my wife or I said anything about all that our members were doing for us, they kept saying, "You two are

You need a support group around
you when you're going through.
Do you know who you can call?

always here for us, and now it's our time to be there for you." I still cry when I think about how much others cared about us and cared for us in our time of need.

We met with the hospital staff, and on the sixth afternoon they encouraged us to go home for the night and to return at noon the following day. We slept at home for the first time in five nights.

> *I realised that God has placed Christians everywhere, to support each other, to support the needy in those areas, and that is the thing that I find is a great plus.*
>
> Cliff Richards

CHAPTER 5.

SLEEPING AT HOME FELT DIFFERENT

How can you sleep after suffering one of the worst types of pain a parent could face? How do you close your eyes and rest knowing that someone hurt your baby girl? Sleeping was extremely hard for me, and I don't know if you have had to experience it, but my prayer is for you to sleep better.

Our home just didn't feel right without Cuppie. Have you ever tried sleeping at home while a loved one was on life support in a trauma center? It's almost impossible to sleep soundly, and when you do sleep, you have dreams about your loved one. Dreams that seem so real they you wake up!

On the morning of June 10, 2015, as we were preparing to go back to the hospital, I received a call that our beloved Cuppie had passed. I believe now that when they asked us to go home the night before, they knew this might happen. We cried, and family members who were at our house were weeping because she was gone. A stranger just entered our family circle and took our Beloved Cuppie away.

From the night of June10th until June 18th, our house was packed with people. Some were

"Whatever you've been through,
I've found that being alone with nothing to
do will make things worse."

people I knew, and others I didn't know. They knew us, or they knew Lorraine and wanted to support our family. Lorraine was very well popular, and I must say that we had more food, water, and sodas that came every day and night. We had so much that, again, we had to share with others.

To me having a packed house was good because I love people, and I needed them to lean on for support. I dreaded seeing them leave every night; but eventually they were all gone.

When tragedies like this happen, people will promise to check on you, but not really follow through. In their defense, they just say anything at that time to make you feel like you're not alone. Many really don't know what to say, so they just say what they hear others say or what they think you need to hear.

Don't be upset with them. They tried. After a while, they almost forget about comforting you because of their busy lives.

I started to think about words that I've said to people when they experienced a loss; and I really saw how powerful spoken words are. The right words spoken with good intentions can provide support and comfort, but with no follow-through, they become tools that Satan will use to torment the person who is already suffering.

I thought about words and phrases that I have told people to ease their pain over my many years in ministry, and now I was on the receiving end of words or phrases such as;

- "I will always be there for you."
- "Whatever you need just let me know."
- "Just say it, and you got it."
- "I'm in this with you until the end."
- "We are like family."
- "I will check on you at least once per week."
- "Is there anything that you need?"

I accept that most people don't know how long these words should last. How long should they keep calling? Should they stop by weekly? Monthly? How much contact is too much contact? Should they bring up the deceased? I am learning to let people off the hook with their promises after a tragedy occurs because most just don't know what is appropriate after a child is killed. Choose to think the best of your friends and family. They love you and want to help.

Whatever you have been through, I've found out that being alone with nothing to do will make things worse. If you haven't already done so, get spiritual counseling; attend group sessions with others who have suffered your kind of pain; pray, study the Bible, get a hobby, etc., but please don't sit there and waste away. Don't let negative thoughts run wild in your mind.

I struggled with being productive after losing our beloved Cuppie, and when I just sat there, I was miserable. Don't just sit alone. Remember, *"The LORD is close to the brokenhearted and saves those who are crushed in spirit"* (Psalms 34:18).

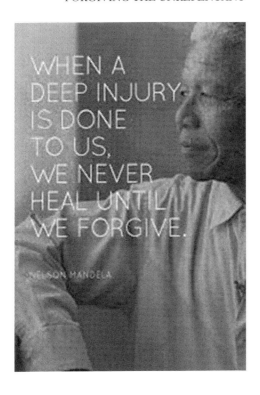

CHAPTER 6.
INTERVIEW WITH THE NEWS

We were asked about doing an interview with the news, and we accepted. Again, so many things happened so fast that you just cannot prepare for it all.

The interview happened at our house on June 12th, two days after our beloved daughter passed. We sat in our house, in front of a camera, and we were asked questions by a reporter. I personally had no idea what I was going to say. Trust me, the Lord will speak through you, and whatever is in you will come out.

The Word that I hid in my heart came out. There was no pre-interview-- everything was live. My wife spoke about Lorraine first, and then it was my turn. I have been taught. I have and still do preach and teach to others, and although I was hurt beyond description, the words of life on the inside of me just began to flow out of my mouth. Luke 6:45 explains it this way, *"The good man, out of the good treasure stored in his heart brings forth that which is good; and the evil man out of the evil stored in his heart, brings for that which is evil; for out of the abundance of the heart his mouth speaks."* If you cuss and fuss that's what will come out of your mouth under pressure, but when you are a new creature in Christ, old things are passed away. **I said that I forgive the woman who did this senseless thing to our daughter. I've always been taught to hate the sin and love the sinner, and it just came out.**

I was forgiving an unrepentant person, a person who has never said that she was sorry for taking my child's life. I was choosing to forgive her. Let me be perfectly clear; I was not releasing her from her punishment on earth. When a person commits a crime on earth, the person should expect to face the consequences of the criminal justice system.

My giving forgiveness freed me from holding a grudge. My giving forgiveness freed me from retaliating. My giving forgiveness allowed me to continue to go through this- knowing that I would never totally get over it- without becoming bitter.

I would be wrong if I didn't repeat this. Who can tell someone to get over a major loss? Wake up! Some things people will never get over, but with the help of the Lord they can walk in the valley of the shadow of death and come out on the other side.

What would it benefit me to hate the woman who killed my daughter? Are you walking around with hate in your heart? Are you benefiting from walking around with hatred in your heart? I know I've said it before, but it bears repeating: **We can't control what someone does or says to us, but we can, with the help of the Holy Ghost, control our reactions and behavior.**

I don't know the woman, and I don't think we will ever talk, based on her actions that I have seen, so my choice through the power of God the Father, Son and Holy Ghost was to forgive her. Yes, I was angry, but I chose not to sin. I could not do what others thought that I should do because of who I am, and to Whom I belong. The One who sits high and looks low will avenge me as He sees fit! He will avenge you too.

If you have a grudge in your heart against someone, you're hurting yourself because they have probably moved on in life. We can never, and I mean never, control what another person does or says out of their mouth; however, we can choose to let the Word of God govern how we will behave. Remember Psalms 18. When you call to God, He will come to you and avenge you against your enemies.

There is no need to add fuel to a fire that will only end up consuming you, and possibly destroying your life. Love covers a multitude of sins. I want to speak to your heart right now. It's time for you to forgive. Stop holding that grudge. Whatever has happened can't be changed. I know that you will never forget it, but you must live.

What are ways that holding on to unforgiveness has hurt you? Has unforgiveness hurt your family or friends?

Do know that unforgiveness is classified as a disease in medical books? According to Dr. Steven Standiford, chief of surgery at the Cancer Treatment Centers of America, "refusing to forgive makes people sick and keeps them that way." Cancer is the leading disease strengthened by unforgiveness.

"Harboring these negative emotions; the anger, hatred, [unforgiveness], creates a state of chronic anxiety... chronic anxiety very predictably produces excess adrenaline and cortisol, which deplete the production of natural killer cells, which is your body's foot soldier in the fight against cancer," explained Dr. Michael Berry, author of *The Forgiveness Project.*

Forgive anyone
who caused you pain or harm.

Keep in mind that
forgiving is not for others.
It is for you. Forgiving is not
forgetting. It is remembering
without anger. It frees up
your power, heals your body,
mind and spirit. Forgiveness
opens up a pathway to a new
place of peace where
you can persist despite what
has happened to you.

Les Brown.

CHAPTER 7.
MAKING ARRANGEMENTS FOR THE HOMEGOING

I sold life insurance for years after I retired from the United States Army. I also worked for a funeral home where I sold burial plots, mausoleums, funeral plans and more, but dealing with the burial of my child was different. I was sitting on the other side of

"If you have a grudge in your heart against someone, you're hurting yourself because they have probably moved on in life."

the table and it was *my* daughter who was deceased. Sitting and answering questions from a funeral director for the loss of a child is extremely hard. We had everything in place regarding insurance coverage, but we never thought we would need it. I didn't think in a million years that we would ever have to make funeral arrangements for our child.

If you ever have to go through this, and I pray that you won't, trust in the Lord for your steps to be ordered by Him. I've heard many say that they can't do it, but with God all things are possible. God will give you the strength when you need it.

Maybe it wasn't the loss of a child that you suffered; but it's something you feel like you can't handle. I'm here on assignment from God to let you know that you can make it. We had to pick the date of the service, flowers, casket, clothing and more for our daughter, and the pain seemed unbearable, but God and our friends helped us get through.

On a more practical note, one of the most important things you must do to protect your family is to make sure that you have life insurance. Not having the resources to pay for the necessary expenses during a time of unexpected loss would have been too much to handle for us; so, we were financially prepared. We had what we needed, and this gave us peace to focus on our family, especially on little PaPa. Do you have insurance on all your loved ones? If not, please speak with a licensed agent immediately, and protect your family!

Forgiveness is not an occasional act, it is a permanent attitude

- Martin Luther King Jr. -

CHAPTER 8.
PRAYER VIGIL

S

o many things happened quickly. O n June 18, 2015, hundreds of family and friends packed the street corner in our neighborhood for a prayer vigil for Lorraine. Prayer vigils happen all over America, and I've watched, attended, prayed for and participated in many; but I never imagined that there would be one for my child!

"I didn't think, even though we had life insurance coverage,

that we would ever have to make arrangements

for our child. No parent should have to bury

their child!"

My wife and I decided not to go to the scene of the crime because we just could not handle that. I've heard that to get over something, you must go to the place that it happened. I'm not sure that's always a good idea. Why go back to the place that caused you so much emotional damage? I'd rather forget those things that are behind and press on in life!

Everyone must do what is best for them. Don't let anyone force you to do something that you aren't ready to do. You know what you can and cannot handle; just as you know when you can handle certain things. Trust that the Holy Ghost will lead you when and where you need to go by giving you His peace. If you don't have peace about something, don't do it! I never have been to the scene of the crime since the incident happened, and I don't intend on going any time soon. I have peace about that, and I trust God to not place any more on my family than we can bear.

There were so many people at the prayer vigil that I can't name them all, but I do say thank you to them all and God bless them all. Going to a prayer vigil for your loved one is very hard because you really are hurting so bad. All you really want to do is scream and holler as loud as you can, but you don't. If you ever have to go to a prayer vigil for a family member or friend, please do go because prayer is a powerful tool that can and will cause change. One of my favorite sayings is "Prayer can go where we can't go!"

James 5:16 in the Amplified Bible confirms this,

"Therefore, confess your sins to one another [your false steps, your offenses], and pray for one another, that you may be

healed and restored. The heartfelt and persistent prayer of a righteous man (believer) can accomplish much [when put into action and made effective by God—it is dynamic and can have tremendous power].

I spoke during the vigil to reporters about the city of Savannah. I feel that it's a very good city-- full of people who will rally around you in the time of need. I also feel that no act of violence can outweigh love. The city of Savannah has problems like most cities, but its people rallied behind my family, and me; and I am eternally grateful.

"I've heard that to get over something, you must go to the place that it happened. I'm not sure that's always good. Why go back to the place that caused you so much emotional damage? I'd rather forget those things that are behind and press on in life!"

A PRAYER OF FORGIVENESS

If someone has hurt you in the past, and you never forgave them, then I want to offer you this prayer from Volume One *of Prayers That Avail Much* by Germaine Copeland that will let you release yourself from the bondage of unforgiveness.

Father, in the name of Jesus, I make a fresh commitment to You to live in peace and harmony, not only with the other brothers and sisters of the Body of Christ, but also with my friends, associates, neighbors, and family.

Father, I repent of holding on to bad feelings towards other. I bind myself to godly repentance and loose myself from bitterness, resentment, envying, strife, and unkindness in any form.

Father, I ask Your forgiveness for the sin of _____. By faith, I receive it, having assurance that I am cleansed from all unrighteousness through Jesus Christ. I ask You to forgive and to release all who have wronged and hurt me. I forgive and release them. Deal with them in Your mercy and lovingkindness.

From this moment on, I purpose to walk in love, to seek peace, to live in agreement, and to conduct myself toward others in a manner that is pleasing to You. I know that I have right standing with You and Your ears are attentive to my prayers.

It is written in Your Word that the love of God has been poured forth into my heart by the Holy Ghost, Who is given to me. I believe that love flows forth into the lives of everyone I know, that I may be filled with and abound in the fruits of righteousness, which bring glory and honor unto You, Lord, in Jesus' name. So be it! Amen.

Scripture References

Romans 12:16-18	Mark 11:25
Romans 12:10	Ephesians 4:32
Philippians 2:2 1	Peter 3:8, 11-12
Ephesians 4:31	Colossians 1:10
Ephesians 4:27	Romans 5:5
John 1:9	Philippians 1:9, 11

CHAPTER 9.

THE HOMEGOING SERVICE

Have you ever had to attend a service for someone who died an unexpected, tragic and senseless death? If you haven't, I pray that you never have to go through it. My daughter was young, well-loved, and she had many friends; so, we needed a place large enough to accommodate family, friends and others. I thank God that Bishop Matthew Odum and The Temple of Glory family opened their doors for us.

There are some debts that you can never repay, and I'm so thankful that during this awful time, no one helped my family and I for reciprocity's sake. We were surrounded with people whose only goal was to love, comfort, support, and help us. For that, my family and I are blessed and very grateful.

Everything happened so fast that day. We had a police escort from our house by the Savannah Chatham Metro Police Department. My family and I are so thankful for the Presidential convoy to the church and to the cemetery they provided for our Cuppie. Once we arrived, the entire service seemed to just fly by like the wind. Here I was, sitting in an unfamiliar place, on the front row, with my wife, my son, our grands, and family. I was in a place that I

*"There are things that you can never repay people for giving,
and I'm so thankful that people don't do things
for reciprocity's sakes."*

had never imagined—could not have imagined. Have you ever been in a place like that? My pastor preached an awesome message about numbering your days. Thank you, Pastor Thomas E. Williams!

After the service, we went to Hillcrest Abbey West, a place where I worked, and we placed Lorraine's remains in the top of a mausoleum. She was entombed because there was no way that I was going to place her remains in the ground. As hard as this was to do, I knew that we had to trust God. We found solace in 1 Thessalonians 4:13-18, which says, *"Brothers and sisters, we do not want you to be uniformed about those who have died so you will not grieve like people who have no hope. For since we believe that Jesus died and was raised to life again, we also believe that when Jesus returns, God will bring back with Him the Believers who have died… and the dead in Christ will rise first… so encourage each other with these words."*

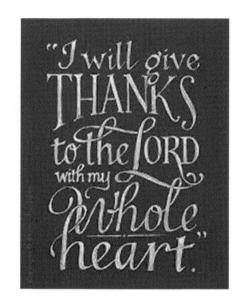

CHAPTER 10.
GOING TO COURT

Waiting for the trial to begin was taxing on us, but we were patient.

Unfortunately for us, the woman who murdered our daughter was walking around free wearing an ankle monitor rather than being locked up in a jail cell like most people accused of murder. This was I believe because of her age—she was elderly. Just know that older people do stupid, senseless things too.

The fact that she wasn't in jail until the trial was something that Satan used to try to make us bitter. He wanted us to meditate on the injustice of that. Thankfully, the Holy Ghost would not let us think that way for long!

He brought several scriptures to our mind that reminded us of the following:

- *"I will get revenge and pay them back [says the LORD] at the time their foot slips; for the day of their disaster is near, and the impending judgment is rushing upon them"* (Deuteronomy 32:35 New English Translation Bible).

- *"Do not repay anyone evil for evil; consider what is good before all people. If possible, so far as it depends on you, live peaceably with all people. Do not avenge yourselves, dear friends, but give place to God's wrath, for it is written, 'Vengeance is mine, I will repay,' says the Lord"* (Romans 12:17-19 New English Translation).

That's what being in a relationship with God will do for you. He will lead you to think and act like Jesus, if you submit to Him rather than to your feelings.

Once, while I was waiting on my wife, I saw the woman going into the store where my wife was. All I could do was pray that my wife didn't see her. When my wife returned to the car, I drove off; and later when we were far away, I asked her if she saw the woman; and she said no. Trust me; it was good that she didn't because we know that the spirit is willing, but the flesh is weak (Matthew 26:41).

What would you do if you saw the person who took the life of your loved one? Would you do them bodily harm? You're probably thinking, *"Come on man, you must have wanted to hurt her."* Did I want to jump out of the car and choke her? No! Why not? She was insignificant after I forgave her. That is so powerful that it bears repeating: **SHE WAS**

INSIGINIFICANT AFTER I FORGAVE HER!

You will either respond fleshly or spiritually based on how you have trained yourself in the past to behave. If you train yourself to respond based on the scriptures when the little things in life happen to you, then you will respond based on the scriptures when big things happen to you; but if you give in to your flesh when little things happen, you will give in to your flesh when the big things happen. Do you notice the pattern? Your daily preparation will determine how you will respond to difficulties in life.

The Apostle Paul said in 1 Corinthians 9:27, *"I discipline my body like an athlete, training it to do what it should. Otherwise, I fear that after preaching to others I myself might be disqualified."* It's your choice about how you respond in the day of testing. Evil is always present when you want to do what is right, but so is God. If you are a born-again believer, then greater is He who lives in you than the enemy that lives in the world (1 John 4:4).

The trial began, and the first time that I laid eyes on the jury, I knew that things would be tough. One juror was late and lied about why he was late which led to him being reprimanded, replaced and ordered to stay for the entire trial.

Some jurors wouldn't even look up to see what was going on with the witnesses. One juror waited until it was deliberation time and said that she couldn't be a juror because it was against her religion or something. Why didn't she say that in the beginning of the jury selection process? It was a mess!

The prosecutor, Assistant District Attorney, Jerry Rothschild was serious and focused. His staff kept us comfortable. Witnesses told lies, and we just sat and watched as the defense attorney brought up liar after liar. One witness lied about the woman's shirt being torn; and we could do nothing except sit there knowing that he was lying.

The woman on video had already stated that my daughter never touched her, and when the woman came out of the house, she didn't have on a shirt, so we knew he was lying. It seemed like a circus of liars—one after the other; and we were forced to endure it. This was another area that Satan wanted us to become bitter about, but with the help of God we did not take his bait of offense.

This was not television; this was real life. On tv shows I saw people jump over the wall and attack the person who hurt their loved one, but we knew that was not an option for us. What would that have done for our representation of Jesus and to our testimony? You must learn to turn the other cheek! That's right. Don't do what others think that you should do; do what would be pleasing in the sight of the Lord. Elder Cazzie Russell (former NBA player) and my brother-in-law, Pastor Charles Roberson were there along with others to support us. Elder Cazzie continued then and now to offer words of encouragement.

One thing that we learned by going through all of this is that what's printed in the newspaper isn't always totally true. Reporters from the newspaper sat in the courtroom, and they wrote things one-sided all week. I hardly ever read the newspaper since I witnessed that. The sad part is that people were on social media commenting about this case based on the lies told in the newspapers. They had no clue what they were talking about, yet they spoke as if they were there in person to see what happened. This is sad that our world has become a place where people love lies more than the truth.

The trial ended after seven days in a mistrial or hung jury. I have no idea why, after listening to all the evidence, they deliberated for three days. The headline in the paper was a mistrial, and a time was set for a retrial.

I looked at the woman and her family periodically

You must be strong and avoid commenting,
especially when you know the truth!

during the trial, and she had a little smile on her face, but I didn't let it bother me because I knew that she wasn't going to get away with it. After the verdict, the devil said, "Grab her and choke her", but I submitted to the Word of God in James 4:7, and resisted Satan. I smiled, and I shook the devil off. I'm a child of the King, and "No weapon that is formed against me shall prosper!"

We all went our separate ways after talking to Mr. Rothschild, but I was confident that at the next trial she would be found guilty. Someone may have hurt you and they are walking around free; just know that It's not over, until God says that it's over! Many people didn't know what to say; and we just carried on with our life-- waiting for the retrial.

The retrial came, and I immediately saw a more professional looking jury. They were well-dressed and groomed, and they looked like they were ready for duty. They all kept their heads up, and I just knew that the woman would be found guilty and sentenced.

The defense attorney didn't have anything and kept trying to make something out of nothing. The woman murdered my daughter in cold blood, and she tried to cover it up; but this time there would be no hung jury. Surprisingly the newspapers didn't cover the story much—I think it's because they saw that the defense was in trouble.

There were the same lying witnesses and no evidence. Assistant DA, Rothschild was more ready than before, and the case was clearly cut-and-dry. There were two days of testimony; the attorneys gave their closing arguments on the morning of the third day; the jury received instructions from the judge; there was a lunch break; the jury came back and reached a verdict in less than one hour. Guilty on all counts! The woman was sentenced the same day to Life plus 20 years. We cried because of all the emotions that we had held in for years. Our daughter would receive the best justice possible. Her murderer would lose almost all her freedoms and be locked up for the foreseeable future.

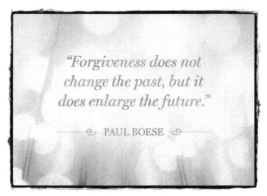

"Forgiveness does not change the past, but it does enlarge the future."

⸻ PAUL BOESE ⸻

FINAL THOUGHTS

I t is often said that many couples end up divorcing after the death of a child. I remember reading somewhere that about every 15

seconds, someone gets divorced for other reasons—with second and third marriages ending in divorce more often.

I'm not sure why that would happen, but I do know that it is very important that when you're going through tragedies in your life, that in addition to turning to God for strength; you turn to your spouse. Lean on each other more during this time.

Try not to judge one another or to put your expectations of how they should act on them. No two people grieve the same, even when they are grieving the same loss. One may be very vocal about how he or she is feeling, while the other may choose quietness. One may express grief in more "traditional" ways like crying; while the other may do things that are a little more eccentric. Let them grieve in their way. It's okay if your spouse needs a little time alone. Pray for him or her. Cover them in heavenly protection more now than ever before.

People grieve in cycles, so don't be surprised if when you finally feel like you're not going to drown in sadness, your spouse may be in that cycle. When your spouse can feel a little peace, you may be in the cycle of anger or depression. It's ok. While you are one in the eyes of God, you are two different people with different grieving cycles. Give each other permission to grieve in the manner and time needed.

There may come a time when one person may want more solitude than the other, and that's ok also. That person may need more self-care. You don't want to be responsible for how anyone else feels— only for your own feelings. You just want to be taken care of and to feel like you will get through to the other side of the pain. It's ok. You are going to make it! You will survive! Your marriage is a wonderful gift that God has given to you, and it will be a source of comfort, protection, safety, and love during times of grief.

You may experience times where dealing with your spouse and family seems unbearable. It is normal, so don't panic. Instead of forcing yourself to talk when you don't want to, try writing down how you feel and let the other read it. Realize that the best way to take care of the marriage is to take care of each person. In Matthew 22:35-40, Jesus said, *"Thou shall love the Lord thy God with all they heart, and with all they soul, and with all they mind. This is the first and great commandment. And the second is like it. You shall love your neighbor as yourself [that is, unselfishly seek the best or higher good for others]. The whole Law and [the writings of the] Prophets depend on these two commandments."* (Amplified Bible) This means that before you can love others, you must love yourself.

Allow each other alone time if it's needed, but also hug and comfort each other if that's what will strengthen your spouse. You both will have to figure out what works for you, and the other must be ok with the fact that this is part of the healing process.

Your feelings will change daily—sometime hourly; and it's okay.

Earlier I used the analogy of drowning because it's one that most people can imagine. Just like the person who is drowning in real life will pull the person trying to rescue him or her under the water, so it is in a marriage when grieving a loss is involved. The person who feels like they are drowning in negative emotions like sadness, despair, anger, depression, etc. will pull his or her rescuer under if they are not careful. I encourage you to share with your spouse when you feel like you're "drowning". Tell each other what you need to feel "rescued" in that moment without pulling the other person down. Choose to look for blessings that you each have. Choose to be kind to one another. Choose to love each other in the way the person needs to feel love rather than the way you need to feel love.

"*Tell each other what you need to feel "rescued" in that moment*"

Sometimes the way a person feels love is very different, so ask them, and choose to really hear them.

If you have other children, remember that they didn't just lose a sibling, they lost the version of parents they had prior to the death. You are not the same person you were prior to the loss that occurred in your life. You look the same on the outside, but you are forever changed on the inside, so don't forget to spend extra time with you other children. Allow them to grieve in their way. Help them express their feelings without judging them. Don't forget them. Ask them what they need from you. I encourage you to listen to them with your heart.

If you have a church family, draw your strength from them. They love you and want to help you as you go through this hardship. Resist thoughts that want you to think you're being a burden because you are not. Your church family loves you, and they want to comfort you. When you hurt, they hurt. So, let them help you.

If you don't have a church family and are near Savannah, Georgia; I invite you to visit our church, Second Ebenezer Baptist Church at 800 Colbert Street Savannah, Georgia 31402. We have services on Sundays at 11am; Sunday School at 9:45 am; and Bible Study & Prayer Meeting on Wednesdays at 7pm. We would love the chance to serve you. Life is too hard to go it alone. At our church, Sinners are Loved; Wounds are Healed; and Needs are Met.

Prayers

The following are prayers that will strengthen your faith. The first time you say them out loud, they are prayers to God. As you continue to say them out of your mouth, they become your confessions of faith that will grow until you manifest them in your daily lives. You only need to confess The Prayer of Salvation once. These prayers/confessions are taken from Germaine Copeland's book, "Prayers that Avail Much" Volumes 1,2, & 3.

To Receive Jesus as Savior and Lord

"Father, it is written in Your Word that if I confess with my mouth that Jesus is Lord and believe with my heart that You have raised Him from the dead, I shall be saved. Therefore, Father, I confess that Jesus is my Lord. I make Him Lord of my life right now. I believe in my heart that You raised Jesus from the dead. I renounce my past life with Satan and close the door to all his devices.

I thank You for forgiving me all my sins. Jesus is my Lord, and I am a new creation. Old things have passed away; now all things become new in Jesus' name. Amen."

Scripture References

John 3:16	John 14:6
John 6:37	Romans 10:9-10
John 10:10	Romans 10:13
Romans 3:23	Ephesians 2:1-10
2 Corinthians 5:19	2 Corinthians 5:17
John 16:8-9	John 1:12
Romans 5:8	2 Corinthians 5:21

Receiving Forgiveness

Father, Your Word declares that if I ask for forgiveness, You will forgive me and cleanse me from all unrighteousness. Help me to believe; help me to receive my forgiveness for past and present sins. Help me to forgive myself. I confess Jesus as my Lord and believe in my heart that You raised Him from the dead, and I am saved.

Father, Your Son, Jesus, said that whatever I ask for in prayer, having faith and really believing, I will receive. Lord, I believe; help my unbelief.

Father, I count myself blessed, how happy I am-- I get a fresh start, my slate's wiped clean. I count myself blessed. You, Father are holding nothing against me, and You're not holding anything back from me.

When I keep it all inside, my bones turn to powder, and my words become daylong groans. The pressure never lets up; all the juices of my life dry up. I am letting it all out; I am saying once and for all that I am making a clean break from my failures to You, Lord.

In the face of this feeling of guilt and unworthiness, I receive my forgiveness, and the pressure is gone—my guilt dissolved, my sin disappeared. I am blessed, for You will never count my sins against me.

"Father, You chose me [actually picked me out for Yourself as Your very own] in Christ before the foundation of the world, that I should be holy (consecrated and set apart for You), blameless in Your sight, even above reproach, before You in love. In Jesus I have redemption (forgiveness) of my offenses (shortcoming and trespasses), in accordance with the riches and the generosity of Your gracious favor.

Lord, I have received Your Son, Jesus; I believe in His name, and He has given me the right to become Your child. I acknowledge You, Lord, as my Father. Thank You for forgiving me and absolving me of all guilt. I am an overcomer by the blood of the Lamb and by the word of my testimony. In the name of Jesus, Amen."

Scripture References

1 John 1:9	Psalm 32:1-6 (Message Bible)
Romans 10:9-10	Romans 4:7-8 (NIV)
Mark 11:23	Ephesians 1:4, 7 (AMP)
Matthew 21:22 (AMP)	John 1:12 (NIV)
Mark 9:24	Revelations 12:11
Psalm 32:1 (AMP)	

Conquering the Thought Life

In the name of Jesus, I take authority over my thought life. Even though I walk and live in the flesh, I am not carrying on my warfare according to the flesh and using mere human weapons. For the weapons of my warfare are not physical (weapons of flesh and blood), but they are mighty before God for the overthrow and destruction of strongholds. I refute arguments and theories and reasoning and every proud and lofty thing that sets itself up against the (true) knowledge of God; and I lead every thought and purpose away captive into the obedience of Christ, the Messiah, the Anointed One.

With my soul [mind, will, and emotions] I will bless the Lord with every thought and purpose in life. My mind will not wander out of the presence of God. My life shall glorify the Father—spirit, soul, and body. I take no account of the evil done to me—I pay no attention to a suffered wrong. It holds no place in my thought life. I am ever ready to believe the best of every person. I gird up the loins of my mind, and I set my mind and keep it set on what is above—the higher things— not on the things that are on the earth.

Whatever is true, whatever is worthy of reverence and is honorable and seemly, whatever is just, whatever is pure, whatever is lovely and loveable, whatever is kind and winsome and gracious, if there is any virtue and excellence, if there is anything worthy of praise, I will think on and weigh and take account of these things—I will fix my mind on them.

I have the mind of Christ, the Messiah, and do hold the thoughts (feelings and purposes) of His heart. In the name of Jesus, I will practice what I have learned and received and heard and seen in Christ and model my way of living on it, and the God of peace—of untroubled, undisturbed wellbeing—will be with me. In Jesus' name, Amen."

Scriptures References

2 Corinthians 10:3-5	Colossians 3:2
Psalm 103:1	Philippians 4:8
1 Corinthians 6:20	1 Corinthians 2:16
1 Corinthians 13:5-7	Philippians 4:9
1 Peter 1:13	

Letting Go of Bitterness

"Father, life seems so unjust and so unfair at times. Help me to let go of all bitterness and indignation and wrath (passion, rage, bad temper) and resentment (anger and animosity).

You are the One Who binds up and heals the broken-hearted. I receive Your anointing that destroys every yoke of bondage. I receive emotional healing by faith, and I thank You for giving me the grace to stand firm until the process is complete.

Thank You for wise counselors. I acknowledge the Holy Spirit as my wonderful Counselor. Thank You for helping me work out my salvation with fear and trembling, for it is You, Father, Who works in me to will and to act according to Your good purpose.

In the name of Jesus, I choose to forgive those who have wronged me. I purpose to live a life of forgiveness because You have forgiven me. With the help of the Holy Spirit, I get rid of all bitterness, rage, anger, brawling, and slander, along with every form of malice. I desire to be kind and compassionate to others, forgiving them, just as in Christ You forgave me.

With the help of the Holy Spirit, I make every effort to live in peace with all men and to be holy, for I know that without holiness no one will see You, Lord. I purpose to see it that I do not miss Your grace and that no bitter root grows up within me to cause trouble.

I will watch and pray that I enter not into temptation or cause others to stumble. Thank You, Father, that You watch over Your Word to perform it and that whom the Son has set free is free indeed. I declare that I have overcome resentment and bitterness by the blood of the Lamb and by the word of my testimony. In Jesus' name, Amen."

Scripture References

Ephesians 4:31 (AMP)	Ephesians 4:31-32 (NIV)
Luke 4:18	Hebrews 12:14-15 (NIV)
Isaiah 10:27	Matthew 26:41
Proverbs 11:14	Romans 14:21
John 15:26 (AMP)	Jeremiah 1:12
Philippians 2:12-13 (AMP)	John 8:36
Matthew 5:44	Revelation 12:11

Always pray to have eyes that
see the best in people,
a heart that
forgives the worst,
a mind that
forgets the bad,
and a soul
that never loses faith in God.

©GodFruits.com

ABOUT Ricardo R. Manuel

Pastor Ricardo R. Manuel (Ricky) is a native of Fayetteville, N.C. In 1969, he joined the Fayetteville Deliverance Evangelist Center under the leadership of the late Bishop James Hilton.

His mother is the late Attie J. McLeary (Fayetteville, N.C.), and his father is the late Rudolph C. Campbell (Colon, Panama).

He married the former Angela Roberson in 1981 and has two children Ricardo E'ron and the late Lorraine Marissa "Cuppie". They have two grandchildren, Malorie Grace Manuel and Hraji Azaiah Franklin.

In 1979, he joined the U.S Army after graduating from high school and served 21 years in Personal Records/Supply/Logistics which culminated in his becoming an Assistant to the Inspector General. He received numerous awards and decorations; and he retired as a Senior Non-Commissioned Officer. He was a logistician with the United States Precision Helicopter Team which won first place in France in 1986 and Castlebury, England in 1989.

In 1992, he became a member of the First African Bapt Church of East Savannah under the leadership of Pasto Thomas E. Williams.

In 1996, he became an ordained deacon at First African Baptist Church of East Savannah. At First African, he also was the president of the Brotherhood Ministry and worked with the brown bag feeding program.

He answered his call to ministry and was licensed December 6, 1998 by Pastor Thomas E. Williams. On April 9, 2000 he was ordained by Pastor Thomas E. Williams and shortly afterwards was called to be the Assistant Pastor of Second Ebenezer Missionary Baptist Church under the leadership of Pastor Harold H. Baker.

In October 2003, he was called as the Pastor of Second Ebenezer Missionary Baptist Church. While he was the Pastor, the following ministries were started:

- the Brotherhood,
- Sisterhood,
- Youth After-School Feeding/Tutoring
- Feeding of the Homeless,

- The Christian Coalition Against Crime

- Matthew 25 Housing and

- Liturgical Dance

In 2010, the Ebenezer Youth Choir competed in the Disney Gospel Fest Competition, in Orlando Florida to the glory of God.

In 2016, he started the Annual Hitch Village/Fred Wessels Revival, which brings former members of the former low-income neighborhoods back to the area to preach. The theme is "Can Any Good Thing Come from There?" 2018 marked the 3rd Annual Revival and the hope is to continue yearly.

He is a 2005 Graduate of St. Leo University where he earned a Bachelor's Degree in Religion.

He is a 2011 graduate of Step Up Savannah's Neighborhood Leadership Academy.

He received an Honorary Doctor of Divinity Degree from BOCM School of the Great Commission & International Bible Institute in 2018.

He is a member of International Church Alliance Network (I.C.A.N.) under the leadership of Bishop Daniel Russell.

He has served as a Board Member of the Savannah Court Appointed Special Advocate (C.A.S.A.) for Children and Chair of the Berean Association's Social Civic Awareness Committee.

He currently serves on the Board of Directors of Matthew 25 Housing and on the Board of Directors of Step Up Savannah.

Above all, he is a born-again, baptized, Holy Ghost Filled, believer, who takes his assignment from the Lord seriously.

Two quotes that he is known for saying are, "Prayer goes where we can't go!" and "Keep up the good works!"